Science Songs

Eight Great Planets!

A Song About the Planets

by Laura Purdie Salas

illustrated by Sergio De Giorgi

Sing along to the tune of

"Where Is Thumbkin?"

Learn about the eight planets in our solar system.

The audio file for this book is available for download at:
http://www.capstonekids.com/sciencesongs

PICTURE WINDOW BOOKS
a capstone imprint

Editor: Jill Kalz
Designers: Abbey Fitzgerald and Lori Bye
Art Director: Nathan Gassman
Production Specialist: Jane Klenk
The illustrations in this book were created digitally.

Picture Window Books
151 Good Counsel Drive, P.O. Box 669
Mankato, MN 56002-0669
877-845-8392
www.picturewindowbooks.com

Printed in the United States of America in North Mankato, Minnesota.
092009
005618CGS10

Library of Congress Cataloging-in-Publication Data
Salas, Laura Purdie.
Eight great planets! : a song about the planets /
by Laura Purdie Salas ; illustrated by Sergio De Giorgi.
p. cm. – (Science songs)
Includes index.
ISBN 978-1-4048-5765-0 (library binding)
1. Planets–Juvenile literature. 2. Planets–Songs and music.
I. De Giorgi, Sergio, ill. II. Title.
QB602.S25 2010
523.2–dc22
2009031941

Thanks to our advisers for their expertise, research, and advice:

Jerald Dosch, Ph.D., Visiting Assistant Professor of Biology
Macalester College

Terry Flaherty, Ph.D., Professor of English
Minnesota State University, Mankato

The sun and the eight planets that circle around it make up our solar system. Some planets are closer to the sun. Some are farther away. But they are all moving through outer space on huge oval paths called orbits. In order from the sun, the planets are Mercury, Venus, Earth, Mars, Jupiter, Saturn, Uranus, and Neptune.

See the planets! See the planets!

In the sky! Use your eyes!

Planets in their orbits

Form our solar system.

Aren't they great? There are eight!

Our sun is a star. It looks bigger than any other star because it's closer to Earth. Each planet's path around the sun is called its orbit.

Mercury is the first planet.

Number one! Near the sun!

Mercury is tiny.

It has many craters

Formed by rocks. It's so hot!

Mercury is covered with thousands of craters. When our solar system was forming, chunks of rock and metal were flying everywhere. Each chunk that hit Mercury left a hole in it.

There are lots of storms on Venus—

Bolts of light shine at night.

It's our second planet,

And although it's cloudy,

Lightning's bright. Dazzling sight!

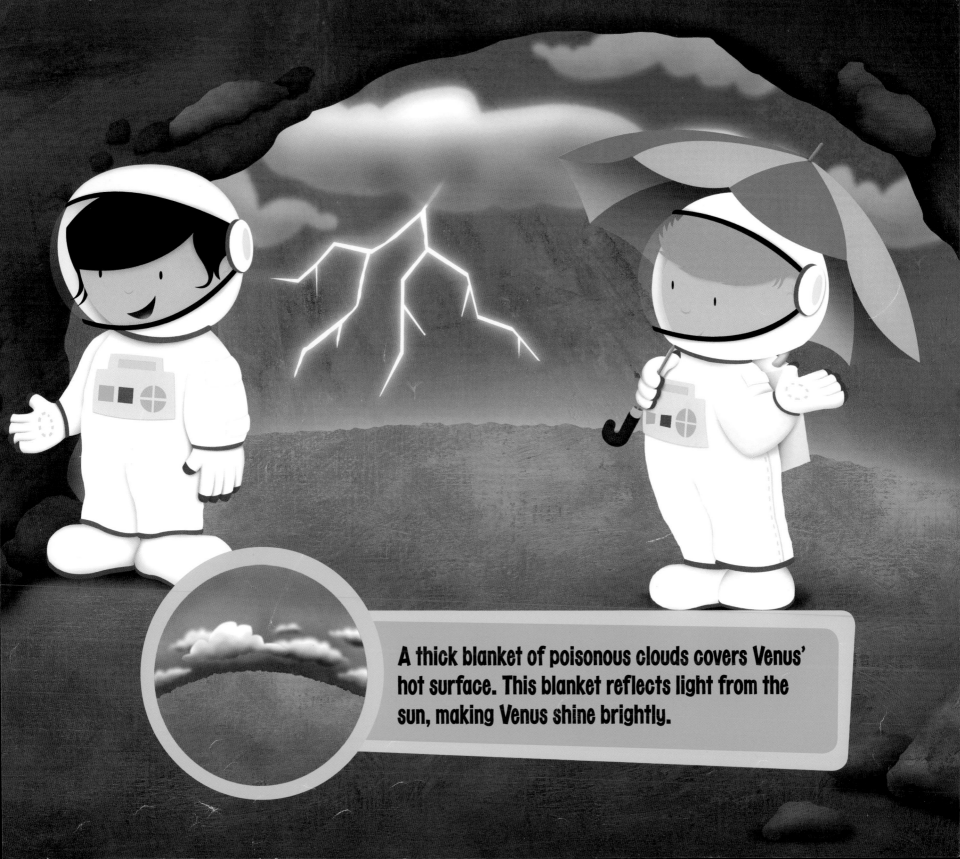

A thick blanket of poisonous clouds covers Venus' hot surface. This blanket reflects light from the sun, making Venus shine brightly.

Earth is next, and it has land and

Lots of sea. Planet three!

Earth is something special.

It has lots of creatures.

Here we roam. This is home!

10

Our planet is the only one in our solar system that has liquid water. Water makes it possible for us to have life on Earth.

Mars comes next. It's the fourth planet.

Red and dry! Mountains high!

Icy layers form at

Both the north and south poles.

We explore. We learn more!

Mars has sheets of ice at its north pole and south pole, just like Earth does. Mars' red color comes from iron in its soil. More spacecraft have been sent to Mars than to any other planet.

Jupiter is the fifth planet.

Made of gas! Has great mass!

Thirteen hundred Earths could

Fit inside this giant.

That is huge. Really huge!

Jupiter is the largest planet in our solar system. Scientists believe Jupiter's Great Red Spot is a storm that has lasted more than 300 years.

Next is Saturn, the sixth planet.

It has rings of ice and things

That circle round the planet.

Strong winds often fan it.

It's big, too. Number two!

The chunks of ice and rock in Saturn's rings are all different sizes. They can be as small as a grain of sand or as big as a school bus.

17

Uranus is planet seven.

Bluish-green! Rings are seen!

It is made of gas, and

Moons float all around it.

Brrr ... it's cold. Freezing cold!

Uranus is bluish-green because of a gas called methane. Uranus has rings, too, like Saturn. It is one of the coldest planets in our solar system.

19

Neptune's last. It's the eighth planet.

Clouds of blue! Nice to view!

We know all our planets,

Sung them all in order,

Just for you. Now we're through!

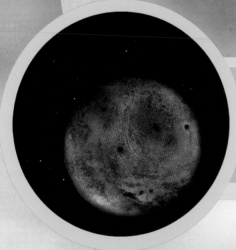

There used to be nine official planets. But in 2006, scientists declared Pluto a "dwarf planet." Now Neptune is the outermost planet of our solar system.

Eight Great Planets!

See the plan-ets! See the plan-ets! In the sky! Use your eyes!

Plan-ets in their or-bits form our so-lar sys-tem. Aren't they great? There are eight!

2. Mercury is the first planet.
Number one! Near the sun!
Mercury is tiny.
It has many craters
Formed by rocks. It's so hot!

3. There are lots of storms on Venus—
Bolts of light shine at night.
It's our second planet,
And although it's cloudy,
Lightning's bright. Dazzling sight!

4. Earth is next, and it has land and
Lots of sea. Planet three!
Earth is something special.
It has lots of creatures.
Here we roam. This is home!

5. Mars comes next. It's the fourth planet.
Red and dry! Mountains high!
Icy layers form at
Both the north and south poles.
We explore. We learn more!

6. Jupiter is the fifth planet.
Made of gas! Has great mass!
Thirteen hundred Earths could
Fit inside this giant.
That is huge. Really huge!

7. Next is Saturn, the sixth planet.
It has rings of ice and things
That circle round the planet.
Strong winds often fan it.
It's big, too. Number two!

8. Uranus is planet seven.
Bluish-green! Rings are seen!
It is made of gas, and
Moons float all around it.
Brrr ... it's cold. Freezing cold!

9. Neptune's last. It's the eighth planet.
Clouds of blue! Nice to view!
We know all our planets,
Sung them all in order,
Just for you. Now we're through!

The audio file for this book is available for download at:
http://www.capstonekids.com/sciencesongs

Did You Know?

The four planets farthest from the sun are called gas planets. Jupiter, Saturn, Uranus, and Neptune are made mostly of gases.

Mars has the largest mountain we know of in our solar system. It's called Olympus Mons. It is three times taller than Mount Everest, the tallest mountain on Earth.

Earth takes 365 days to circle once around the sun. The dwarf planet Pluto takes 248 Earth years to circle just once around the sun.

Mercury can be colder than minus 280 degrees Fahrenheit (minus 173 degrees Celsius) at night. But during the day, it can reach 800 °F (427 °C)!

Glossary

crater—a bowl-shaped hole

dwarf planet—a nearly round object that circles the sun and is not big enough to be a planet, but is too big to be a moon or asteroid

iron—a gray-white metal in some rocks that rusts and turns reddish when air touches it

orbit— the oval-shaped path one object takes around another object in space

solar system—our sun and all the objects that travel around the sun, including the eight planets

23

To Learn More

More Books to Read

Bredeson, Carmen. *What Is the Solar System?* Berkeley Heights, N.J.: Enslow Elementary, 2008.

Kudlinski, Kathleen V. *Boy, Were We Wrong About the Solar System!* New York: Dutton Children's Books, 2008.

Trammel, Howard K. *The Solar System.* New York: Children's Press, 2010.

Internet Sites

FactHound offers a safe, fun way to find Internet sites related to this book. All of the sites on FactHound have been researched by our staff.

Here's all you do:

Visit *www.facthound.com*

FactHound will fetch the best sites for you!

Index

Look for all of the books in the Science Songs series:

♪ Are You Living?
A Song About Living and Nonliving Things

♪ Eight Great Planets!
A Song About the Planets

♪ From Beginning to End:
A Song About Life Cycles

♪ Home on the Earth:
A Song About Earth's Layers

♪ I'm Exploring with My Senses:
A Song About the Five Senses

♪ Many Creatures:
A Song About Animal Classifications

♪ Move It! Work It!
A Song About Simple Machines

♪ There Goes the Water:
A Song About the Water Cycle